Ava DuVernay
Movie Director

by Kate Moening

BLASTOFF! 2 READERS

BELLWETHER MEDIA · MINNEAPOLIS, MN

Blastoff! Readers are carefully developed by literacy experts to build reading stamina and move students toward fluency by combining standards-based content with developmentally appropriate text.

Level 1 provides the most support through repetition of high-frequency words, light text, predictable sentence patterns, and strong visual support.

Level 2 offers early readers a bit more challenge through varied sentences, increased text load, and text-supportive special features.

Level 3 advances early-fluent readers toward fluency through increased text load, less reliance on photos, advancing concepts, longer sentences, and more complex special features.

★ **Blastoff! Universe**

Reading Level

Grade **K**
Grades **1–3**
Grade **4**

This edition first published in 2021 by Bellwether Media, Inc.

No part of this publication may be reproduced in whole or in part without written permission of the publisher. For information regarding permission, write to Bellwether Media, Inc., Attention: Permissions Department, 6012 Blue Circle Drive, Minnetonka, MN 55343.

Library of Congress Cataloging-in-Publication Data
Names: Moening, Kate, author.
Title: Ava DuVernay : movie director / Kate Moening.
Description: Minneapolis, MN : Bellwether Media, 2021. | Series: Blastoff! readers: women leading the way | Includes bibliographical references and index. | Audience: Ages 5-8 | Audience: Grades K-1 | Summary: "Relevant images match informative text in this introduction to Ava DuVernay. Intended for students in kindergarten through third grade"– Provided by publisher.
Identifiers: LCCN 2019053860 (print) | LCCN 2019053861 (ebook) | ISBN 9781644872079 (library binding) | ISBN 9781681038315 (paperback) | ISBN 9781618919656 (ebook)
Subjects: LCSH: Duvernay, Ava–Juvenile literature. | Motion picture producers and directors–United States–Biography. | African American motion picture producers and directors–Biography. | Women motion picture producers and directors–United States–Biography.
Classification: LCC PN1998.3.D9255 M64 2021 (print) | LCC PN1998.3.D9255 (ebook) | DDC 791.4302/33092 [B]–dc23
LC record available at https://lccn.loc.gov/2019053860
LC ebook record available at https://lccn.loc.gov/2019053861

Editor: Elizabeth Neuenfeldt   Designer: Andrea Schneider

Printed in the United States of America, North Mankato, MN.

Table of Contents

Who Is Ava DuVernay?

Ava DuVernay is a movie **director**. She directed *A Wrinkle in Time*!

Ava also writes and **produces** movies. She wants to tell stories about African Americans.

Ava on the set of *A Wrinkle in Time*

Ava grew up in Compton, California. Her aunt Denise taught her to love movies.

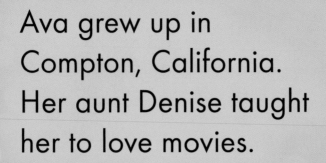

Compton

California

N
W · E
S

Ava with students from
a Compton middle school

Ava's favorite was *West Side Story*.
It made her want to work in movies!

Getting Her Start

Ava on a movie set

After college, Ava did movie **publicity**. Soon she started her own **company**!

Ava visited many **sets**. She saw how movies were made.

Ava DuVernay Profile

Birthday: August 24, 1972

Hometown: Compton, California

Field: film

Schooling:
- studied African American Studies, English

Influences:
- Denise Sexton (aunt)
- Oprah Winfrey (producer, talk show host)

Ava dreamed of making her own films. She started making **documentaries**.

Later, Ava used her savings to direct her first **feature film**!

Changing the World

Many **studios** would not produce Ava's movies. They thought nobody would watch movies made by a black woman.

But Ava knew they were wrong.

13

Ava directed a movie called *Selma*. It was about the **civil rights movement**.

Selma

Ava winning an award for *Selma*

The movie won many **awards**. It made studios listen to Ava!

Growing up, Ava saw few movies about black girls. She wanted to change that.

In 2018, she directed *A Wrinkle in Time*. The movie **included** many people of color.

Ava directing
A Wrinkle in Time

"I BELIEVE THAT GOOD COMES WHEN YOU **PUT OUT GOOD.**" (2014)

17

Ava's Future

Ava is still a director! She wants
to change the movie business.

Ava DuVernay Timeline

2008   Ava directs her first documentary

2010   Ava founds Array, a company that shares movies made by people of color and women

2012   Ava becomes the first black director to win the best director award at the Sundance Film Festival

2015   *Selma* is nominated for Best Picture at the Academy Awards

2018   Ava directs *A Wrinkle in Time*

Ava wants movies to **represent** more people.

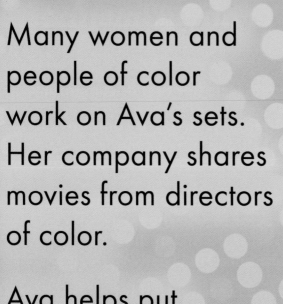

Many women and
people of color
work on Ava's sets.
Her company shares
movies from directors
of color.

Ava helps put
more people in
the spotlight!

"SAY WHAT
YOU ARE.
BE PROUD OF
WHAT YOU ARE."
(2014)

Glossary

awards—rewards or prizes that are given for a job well done

civil rights movement—the national effort in the 1950s and 1960s made by black people and their supporters to gain equal rights

company—a group that makes, buys, or sells goods for money

director—a person who leads people making a movie or show

documentaries—movies or TV shows that tell facts about real people or events

feature film—a full-length movie that tells a story for entertainment

included—made someone a part of something

produces—takes charge and provides the money to make something

publicity—the business of getting people to pay attention to something

represent—to show

sets—places where movies or TV shows are filmed

studios—companies that make movies

To Learn More

AT THE LIBRARY

Bell, Samantha. *You Can Work in Movies*. North Mankato, Minn.: Capstone Press, 2019.

Grabham, Tim. *Video Ideas*. New York, N.Y.: DK Publishing, 2018.

Moening, Kate. *Kathleen Kennedy: Movie Producer*. Minneapolis, Minn.: Bellwether Media, 2020.

ON THE WEB

FACTSURFER

Factsurfer.com gives you a safe, fun way to find more information.

1. Go to www.factsurfer.com.

2. Enter "Ava DuVernay" into the search box and click 🔍.

3. Select your book cover to see a list of related content.

Index

The images in this book are reproduced through the courtesy of: Kathy Hutchins, front cover (Ava), p. 9; gualtiero boffi, front cover, pp. 3, 22; Kit Leong, front cover (city); TCD/Prod.DB/ Alamy, pp. 4 (inset), 16 (inset); Stills Press/ Alamy, pp. 4-5 (main); Jesse Grant/ Stringer/ Getty Images, pp. 6-7 (top); Photo 12/ Alamy, pp. 8-9 (top), 10 (inset), 14; Taylor Hill/ Contributor/ Getty Images, pp. 10-11; PictureLux/ The Hollywood Archive/ Alamy, 12-13 (top); Marla Aufmuth/ Contributor/ Getty Images, p. 13 (bottom); UPI/ Alamy, pp. 14-15 (top); The Photo Access/ Alamy, pp. 16-17; PA Images/ Alamy, pp. 18-19; Invision for Paramount Home Media Distribution/ AP Images, p. 20 (inset); Emma McIntyre/ Staff/ Getty Images, pp. 20-21.